THE LETTER TO THE **HEBREWS**

STUDIES IN THIS SERIES *Available from your Christian bookstore:*

hebrews

THE LETTER TO THE HEBREWS

16 DISCUSSIONS FOR GROUP BIBLE STUDY
MARILYN KUNZ &
CATHERINE SCHELL

TYNDALE HOUSE
PUBLISHERS, INC.
WHEATON, ILLINOIS

Fifteenth printing, July 1986
ISBN 0-8423-1410-5

contents

How to Use
This Discussion Guide

How to prepare to lead a study

1/ Pray for wisdom and the Holy Spirit's guidance.

2/ Read the Bible passage through, thoughtfully, at least twice.

3/ Study the discussion questions and think through the answers as you find them in the passage.

4/ Look over the questions again, and think through how you will rephrase them into your own words. This will help your leadership of the discussion to be truly your own.

5/ Pray for the ability to guide the discussion with love and understanding.

How to lead a study

1/ Begin with prayer for minds open to understand, and hearts willing to obey, the Word of the Lord. You may ask another member of the group to pray if you have asked him ahead of time.

2/ Except during the first study discussion, review the verse(s) memorized from the previous week's study.

3/ Have the Bible chapter read aloud by paragraphs. Be sure to have the reading done by paragraph or thought units, *never* verse by verse. It is not necessary for everyone to read aloud, or for each to read an equal amount.

4/ Guide the group to discover what the passage says by asking the discussion questions. Use the suggestions from the section on "how to encourage everyone to participate."

5/ As the group discusses the Bible passage together, encourage each one to be honest in self-appraisal. You must take the lead in spiritual honesty. Try to avoid hypocrisy in any form.

6/ Bring the discussion to a close at the end of the time allotted, summarizing the impact that this passage can have upon your situation today. You as leader or one of the group members may summarize.

7/ As the leader, read aloud the APPLICATION questions. Encourage everyone in the group to follow the suggestions in this application section during the coming week.

8/ Ask someone in the group to read aloud from a standard translation (Revised Standard Version, New English Bible, Douay Version, or King James Version) the verses to be memorized from this day's study. Encourage the group to commit the verse(s) to memory this week. (If the group is willing to memorize the suggested verses weekly, they will find that this helps them to get and keep a working grasp of the key ideas of this whole book.)

9/ Close in a prayer of thanksgiving or committal.

How to encourage everyone to participate

1/ Encourage discussion by asking several people to contribute answers to a question. "What do the rest of you think?" or "Is there anything else which could be added?" are ways of encouraging discussion.

2/ Be flexible and skip any questions which do not fit into the discussion as it progresses.

3/ Deal with irrelevant issues by suggesting that the purpose of your study is to discover what is *in the passage*. Suggest an informal chat about tangential or controversial issues after the regular study is dismissed.

4/ Receive all contributions warmly. Never bluntly reject what anyone says, even if you think the answer is incorrect. Instead, ask in a friendly manner, "Where did you find that?" or "Is that actually what it says?" or "What do some of the rest of you think?" Allow the group to handle problems together.

5/ Be sure you don't talk too much as the leader. Redirect those questions which are asked you. A discussion should move in the form of an asterisk, back and forth between members, not in the form of a fan, with the discussion always coming back to the leader. The leader is to act as moderator. As members of a group get to know each other better, the discussion will move more freely, progressing from the fan to the asterisk pattern.

6/ Don't be afraid of pauses or long silences. People need time to think about the questions and the passage. Never, *never* answer your own question — either use an alternate question or move on to another area for discussion.

7/ Watch hesitant members for an indication by facial expression or bodily posture that they have something to say, and then give them an encouraging nod or speak their names.

8/ Discourage too talkative members from monopolizing the discussion by specifically directing questions to others. If necessary speak privately to the over-talkative one about the need for discussion rather than lecture in the group, and enlist his aid in encouraging all to participate.

CHART OF THE LETTER TO THE HEBREWS

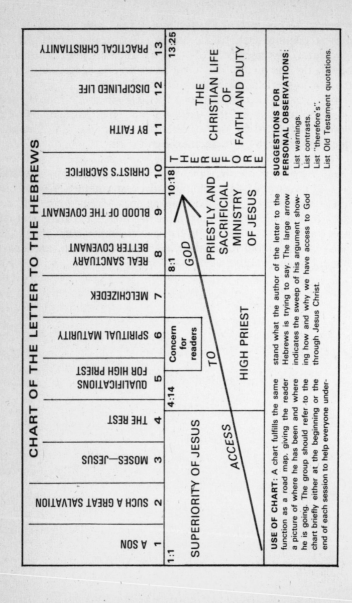

1	2	3	4	5	6	7	8	9	10	11	12	13
A SON	SUCH A GREAT SALVATION	MOSES—JESUS	THE REST	QUALIFICATIONS FOR HIGH PRIEST	SPIRITUAL MATURITY	MELCHIZEDEK	REAL SANCTUARY BETTER COVENANT	BLOOD OF THE COVENANT	CHRIST'S SACRIFICE	BY FAITH	DISCIPLINED LIFE	PRACTICAL CHRISTIANITY

1:1 — 4:14 — 8:1 — 10:18 — 13:25

SUPERIORITY OF JESUS

PRIESTLY AND SACRIFICIAL MINISTRY OF JESUS

THE CHRISTIAN LIFE OF FAITH AND DUTY

GOD

Concern for readers

HIGH PRIEST TO

ACCESS

THEREFORE

USE OF CHART: A chart fulfills the same function as a road map, giving the reader a picture of where he has been and where he is going. The group should refer to the chart briefly either at the beginning or the end of each session to help everyone understand what the author of the letter to the Hebrews is trying to say. The large arrow indicates the sweep of his argument showing how and why we have access to God through Jesus Christ.

SUGGESTIONS FOR PERSONAL OBSERVATIONS:
List warnings.
List contrasts.
List "therefore's".
List Old Testament quotations.

Introduction to the Letter to the Hebrews

The letter to the Hebrews was probably written within the few years immediately preceding the destruction of the Second Temple during the fall of Jerusalem in A.D. 70. From the destruction of that temple to the present day, there has been no regular observance of the sacrificial ritual to which this letter refers many times. The whole question of true religion, how a man may obtain access to God, is at issue in this letter. The writer sets out to prove that the imperfect shadows of the Old Testament sacrificial worship meet perfection and reality in Jesus Christ, the Son of God. Jesus is superior to the Old Testament prophets, to angels, to Moses, to Joshua. He is superior to the Jewish high priest, he is the mediator of a superior covenant, he himself is the perfect sacrifice, his blood is superior to that of bulls and goats. Jesus is the only one who can bring us to spiritual reality and make it possible for us to have access to God.

The letter is punctuated with some of the severest warnings in the whole New Testament, warnings against neglecting the great opportunity made available to us by the Lord Jesus Christ, warnings against looking to the old covenant for a way of salvation now that the true and perfect way has been pioneered for us by Jesus Christ. In this letter we have a literary style which makes it perhaps the most beautiful description of Christianity ever written.

The author is not known. Most present-day scholars believe it was not the apostle Paul. Possibilities include Barnabas, Apollos, and others. The likely destination of the letter was a group of Christian Jews living in a large town in Italy, possibly Rome.

The theme of the letter to the Hebrews is to show that all that the Jewish religion sets forth under the old covenant is fulfilled in the new covenant instituted by Jesus Christ. All that belonged to the old is completely surpassed by the superior quality and reality of the new. It warns that the superiority of this new way of access to God through the blood of Jesus demands a wholehearted and faithful response.

Hebrews 1

God Speaks to Us by a Son

Introduction. In this chapter the writer begins his great theological argument which continues through the middle of chapter 10. He starts by setting forth the unique nature of the Son of God. The fact that angels were considered in Jewish thought as intermediaries between God and man may account for the author's strong emphasis on the position of angels, especially in relation to the Son.

Hebrews 1:1-4

1. What time element is mentioned in verses 1, 2? What exactly is said about God's having spoken through the Old Testament prophets?

2. List eight things which these verses tell about Jesus Christ. Discuss the meaning of each. What benefits does mankind enjoy through the Son?

3. What things are true of the Son which were not true of the prophets? What do the Son and the prophets share in common?

4. Memorize this paragraph. In it we find superbly expressed the most important idea of history.

5. Write out a paraphrase of verses 1-4 in your own words. Then read these verses in J. B. Phillips' translation, *The New Testament in Modern English.*

Hebrews 1:5-14

6. Follow the line of argument through this section (noting the connective words such as *for, or, and, but* will help you do this). What does the writer intend to prove about Jesus

Christ's position in relation to angels?

7. God, not man, is quoted as speaking in verse 5. What do the question and quotations in verse 5 reveal about Jesus? How is Jesus different from, and superior to, both the prophets and the angels?

8. What is your concept of angels? Compare it with what is said about the duties and position of angels in verses 6, 7, 14.

9. What contrast is introduced by "but" at the beginning of verse 8? What responsibilities and authority does the Son have (verses 8, 9)?

10. The Son has been shown to be superior in rank and in power to the prophets and to angels. What is the comparison with the creation itself meant to reveal about the Son in verses 10-12? List the words which describe the creation and those which describe the Son.

11. What thoughts do verses 13 and 14 add to the contrasting functions of angels and the Son, described in verses 7-9? What locations are suggested (verses 13, 14) for the present activities of the Son and of the angels?

12. What relationship do angels have with mankind?

SUMMARY

1. In what ways is the Son superior to the prophets? to angels? to all creation?

2. What is the work attributed to the Son? to God the Father? to the prophets? to the angels?

APPLICATION

Using your answer to summary question number 2 as background, what clues do you see in this chapter as to what God desires men to do?

Memorize Hebrews 1:1-4.

Hebrews 2

Such a Great Salvation

Introduction. Here the writer deals with why the Son of God became man, not angel, and what he accomplished for mankind by doing this.

Hebrews 2:1-4

1. What conclusion does the author of this letter draw from what he has set forth in chapter 1?

2. Describe ways in which a person might "drift away" spiritually? How can we make sure we are not drifting?

3. In Jewish thought, the Old Testament law came through the mediation of angels. In verses 2, 3, what warning is given? On what reasoning is it based?

4. How is the message of the gospel different from the message declared by angels (verses 2-4)? What reasons are given for considering this message to be superior even to the law of Moses?

5. How did the writer and the first readers of this letter hear the gospel?

Hebrews 2:5-9

6. What is the point of the contrast between man and angels in verses 5-8? What does verse 8, commenting on the quotation, emphasize about man? How would *everything* and *nothing outside his control* make clear the position of man in relation to the angels? Compare 1 Corinthians 6:2, 3. What is man's destiny (verses 5-8)?

7. What contrast does the writer draw in saying *we do not yet see . . . but we see?* How does Jesus already fulfill

the destiny of man (verse 9)? Why has Jesus been crowned with glory and honor?

8. What does Jesus share with man? Compare verses 7, 8 with verse 9.

9. What has Jesus done in his death that no other man ever did?

Hebrews 2:10-18

10. The word in verse 10 for *captain* or *pioneer* means leader or originator in the sense of one who initiates and carries through. In what ways was Jesus qualified to be such a pioneer (verses 9a, 11, 14, 18)?

11. Why was it the suffering of Jesus (verse 10) which made him fully adequate for the task of pioneering our salvation?

12. In what ways does the writer further emphasize Jesus' identification with man (verses 11-13 and 14-18)?

13. Keep in mind that it is *the children* of verse 13 who are referred to in verse 14. Consider the reasoning of verses 14, 15. What advantages were obtained by Jesus' taking on full manhood rather than the nature of an angel?

14. Why did Jesus have to die? Discuss the ways in which man expresses his bondage to the fear of death. To what extent are you experiencing the freedom that Christ gives from the fear of death?

15. Note the description of Jesus in his high-priestly position as both *merciful* and *faithful*. What does this mean? Why are both elements necessary? What does Jesus do for men as their high priest (verse 17)? Compare Romans 5:8, 10.

16. What two things has Jesus shared with us (verse 18)? What difference does this make to you?

SUMMARY

1. In your own words describe the *great salvation* set forth in this chapter.

2. What things is Jesus able to do for us? Why?

APPLICATION

Consider the importance of the whole concept of Jesus' identification with man as expressed here. How does our Lord's sympathy and help affect your practical appreciation of your advantages as a Christian? Look for opportunities this week to identify and sympathize with another person for Christ's sake. Consider why you find it difficult to identify with, or be sympathetic to, certain people. Ask the Lord Jesus to change your heart.

Memorize Hebrews 2:9.

Superior to Moses

Introduction. Thus far, the Son is shown to be superior to the Old Testament prophets and to angels. He has taken on flesh and blood and through suffering and death has become an effective high priest in the service of God on behalf of man. Mankind's destiny in God's purpose is revealed to be superior to that of the angels. The writer of this letter now goes on to show that Jesus is superior to the man Moses, whom the Jews considered to have had a unique relationship with God. (See Numbers 12:6-8.)

Hebrews 3:1-6

1. According to 1:1, 2, and 3:1, to whom is this letter addressed?

(Note — The Hebrews to whom this letter was written were Christian believers in danger of being attracted back into Judaism. Therefore, the writer sets out to prove the superiority of Christianity to Judaism by demonstrating how Jesus, the Son of God, surpasses all the messengers and leaders of the old covenant.)

2. What advice does the writer now give on the basis of his argument in chapters 1 and 2?

3. No other New Testament writer calls Jesus an apostle. The writer to the Hebrews calls no other man an apostle. *Apostle* means one who is sent forth upon a special mission, an ambassador. Describe the characteristics of a competent earthly ambassador. How do they apply to Jesus as God's ambassador?

4. What is the meaning of the other title given to Jesus in

verse 1? What two elements in the ministry of Jesus are expressed by the terms *apostle* and *high priest?*

5. In what ways is Jesus shown to be superior to Moses (verses 3-6)? Compare with Hebrews 1:8-12. Consider the importance of the difference shown between Moses and Jesus in verses 5, 6. Compare with Hebrews 1:1, 2.

6. What difference should a realization of these things make to the reader? What is the meaning of the condition stated in verse 6?

7. What would it mean to you to fulfill these conditions? Describe the person who fails to meet these conditions. Read verse 6 from several different translations.

Hebrews 3:7-19

8. What warning is added to verse 6 by the quotation from Psalm 95 in verses 7-11? See Exodus 17:1-7 and Numbers 20:1-13 for two separate events referred to in the Psalms quotation.

(Note — In Hebrews 3:8, 9, *provocation* (*rebellion*) and *temptation* (*testing*) are translations of the Hebrew words Meribah and Massah.)

9. What did the people in the wilderness do wrong (verses 8-10; Exodus 17:3, 7; Numbers 20:3-5, 10, 11)? What was the result for them (verse 11; Numbers 14:22, 23; 20:12)?

10. Those who have become the people of God through faith in Christ are compared to those delivered from Egypt under Moses' leadership. Note the "if" clauses in 2:3; 3:6; 3:14. What does each of these statements stress? What does the writer hold to be imperative?

11. What warning and command are given in verses 12 and 13? What dangers do Christians face? Describe the character and the results of sin (verse 13). What responsibility do Christians have for one another? In what practical ways can we exhort or encourage one another?

12. How may a person become hardened in heart? What warning is implied by the expression *as long as it is called "today"?*

13. What point is being made by the series of questions in verses 16-18? What conclusion is drawn in verse 19? How

does this tie in with the warning in verse 12? What lesson are we to learn from the experience of these Israelites? What is the fatal peril of which we must beware?

SUMMARY

1. Describe the position of Jesus in relation to that of Moses. In what respects does Jesus excel Moses?

2. What responses did God require of his people in the time of Moses? How are Israel's experiences in the wilderness used to warn Christians?

3. What are some of the ways in which the local church, a congregation of Christians, can strengthen one another spiritually to be *holy brethren* following a *heavenly calling?*

APPLICATION

It was the sin of grumbling of which the children of Israel were guilty at Meribah and in other incidents in the wilderness. How can we help children and young people to realize that grumbling is a form of rebellion against the Lord? Why is it important to realize that the majority of the nation under Moses did not believe God?

Memorize Hebrews 3:1.

The Rest Which Is Still Available

Introduction. In the previous chapter, it has been shown how Jesus, the Son of God and builder of God's house, is superior to Moses who was a servant in God's house and also was a part of that house. Also revealed was the tragic example of the Israelites who, though delivered from Egyptian bondage through Moses, failed to enter the land of Canaan. In chapter 4, the writer continues to think of the history of the Jewish people and their failure to enter into the rest God provided.

Hebrews 4:1-10

1. As the writer continues to comment on the application of the warnings and judgments of Psalm 95:7-11, what does he say about *his rest* in verse 1? What does he mean by this phrase? Why must it mean something more than entering into the promised land? Against what danger does he warn?

2. For what the *gospel* (*good news*) is that came to us (verse 2), see Hebrews 2:9, 14, 15, 18.

3. Why didn't the good news of the opportunity to enter Canaan do any good to those who lived in the time of Moses?

4. Being exposed to the message of the gospel is not enough in any generation. Describe the various ways in which a man may react upon hearing the good news.

What response of faith is necessary on our part for us to receive the benefits of the good news that Jesus went through death for us? What relation does action or obedience have to faith? See Hebrews 3:18, 19.

5. Using several of the newer translations, outline the rea-

soning in verses 3-9 by which the writer presents his thought that there is a rest for the people of God (verse 9) entered by faith (verse 3). What indicates that the inheritance of the land of Canaan into which Joshua led Israel was not all that was meant by the promised rest of God (verses 7, 8)?

6. According to verse 10, what does entering God's rest mean for the believer? Compare Ephesians 2:8-10.

7. How are the great promises and intentions of God limited? Why? What responsibility does the individual have?

Hebrews 4:11-13

8. According to verse 11, what should be our response to the warning in verse 1? Compare verse 11, *Let us strive (labor, make every effort) to enter that rest . . .* with verse 3a. How can the elements of rest and striving co-exist? In what sense is there a completion as suggested in verse 3a, and continued action as suggested in verse 11? Give examples of these contrasts in the Christian life.

9. To what kind of *disobedience (example of unbelief)* does verse 11 refer?

10. Read aloud verse 12 from two or three different translations. List at least four things you learn about God's word. What is the meaning of each of these qualities?

11. Give an example from history that God's word is active — namely, that when men take it seriously, things begin to happen. Why must true Bible study always result in action?

12. What does the expression *sharper than any two-edged sword* imply about the nature of God's word? What things does this sword accomplish? How does the word of God help to clarify our true motives?

13. Note the connection in thought between verses 11 and 12. Why must our total inner life (emotional and intellectual) be subject to the penetrating evaluation of God as revealed in his word?

14. How is man's utter transparency before God described (verse 13)? By what means do we try to disguise ourselves before others, or even before ourselves? Compare verse 13 with Psalm 139:7-16. What do both passages teach about God's knowledge of man?

15. What six things are said of Jesus in verses 14-16? Contrast the description of Jesus in verse 14 with that in verse 15.

16. What two things are we to do because we have such a high priest as Jesus? What will it mean in practice for you to do these two things? What reasons are given to encourage this behavior?

SUMMARY

1. What incentive does this chapter offer for living the life of faith? What clues are given here as to how to enter into God's rest?

2. Describe the character of God and the qualities of his word as set forth in this chapter.

3. What weight does 4:12, 13 add to the exhortations in 3:12; 4:1, 11?

4. The main theme of this letter is stated in 4:14-16. Put it briefly into your own words.

5. Turn to the chart of this book on page 10 and locate today's study section in the framework of the letter. Note that we have finished the first major section describing the superiority of Jesus and we have begun the section concerning Jesus as our high priest.

During the coming week you may wish to add your own titles to the different chapters studied thus far and to fill out the part of the chart reserved for personal observations. If necessary, use an additional sheet of paper for these observations.

APPLICATION

In commenting on this chapter William Barclay says: "The fact that Jesus was without sin necessarily means that he knew depths and tensions and assaults of temptation which we never know and never can know. . . . We are easily vanquished; we never know temptation at its fiercest and its most terrible, because we fall long before that stage is reached. But Jesus was tempted as we are — and far beyond what we are." Consider how you can meet each temptation this week in the overcoming power of the Lord Jesus.

Memorize Hebrews 4:12, 13.

Qualifications
for High Priest

Introduction. In this chapter the author goes on to develop the thought introduced in 4:14, that Jesus is our great high priest. Here comparison is made between Jesus and Aaron, the first high priest of Israel.

Hebrews 5:1-10

1. What do you learn about a high priest in verses 1-4 as to his work, his attitudes, and his appointment to office? Why was it important that every Jewish high priest was *chosen from among men?* What offering was required of the high priest (verse 3), but not of Jesus? For why, see 4:15.

2. How does each of the above mentioned requirements for a high priest find perfect fulfillment in Jesus (verses 5-10)? After whose priesthood was that of Jesus patterned? More is said about this in chapter 7.

3. Compare verse 7 with Matthew 26:36-46. Why does the writer believe the prayers of Jesus were answered? For evidence from the Gospels that Jesus' prayers were answered, see Matthew 28:5-7 and Mark 16:6, 7.

4. How does Hebrews 5:8 clarify Hebrews 2:10? Read also Philippians 2:5-11. Suggest ways in which learning comes through suffering. Give examples of how the obedience of godly men in the Old Testament was tested and refined through suffering.

5. For what did all that Jesus experienced fit and equip him? Why is he able to be our Savior? What condition for salvation is stated in verse 9? What is the point of using the word *eternal* to describe the salvation for which Jesus is the source?

Why can nothing in this life or the next change this?

(Note — verse 9 — *being made perfect* — The Greek word for *perfect* used here means to carry out exactly the purpose for which something is designed and made. The experiences that Jesus suffered perfectly fitted him to become the Savior and Redeemer of men.)

6. What important element about the Melchizedek priesthood is revealed in verse 6? How does this substantiate the use of the word *eternal* in verse 9? How long did Aaron's priestly work last?

Hebrews 5:11-14

7. What is the writer's twofold frustration at this point in his presentation? Why, do you think, didn't the writer to the Hebrews close his letter here since he was faced with these difficulties? What remedy is there for us personally when we are tempted to quit because a problem is difficult, or those whom we are seeking to help are unappreciative?

8. What evidence is there that these people have refused to grow up? Why do they need their spiritual ABC's rehearsed again? Compare with the condition of the Corinthian Christians as described in 1 Corinthians 3:1-4.

9. What evidence is there in our generation that spiritual immaturity is still a problem in the church? What signs do you see that Christians are refusing to grow up in knowledge and in behavior? What would you consider as evidence of spiritual maturity?

10. From verses 12-14 describe spiritual maturity.

SUMMARY

1. Describe briefly the qualifications and preparation of Jesus to be our great high priest. Because he is our high priest, what specific blessings and benefits do we enjoy as Christians? Why do we need his work as high priest?

2. List the characteristics of spiritual maturity seen from this chapter. Evaluate yourself by this list.

APPLICATION

Accept the challenge of the writer in verses 11-14, and determine to give eager, thoughtful devotion to the study of the remaining portion of this letter. Be diligent in your personal preparation for the group discussion of each chapter.

Memorize Hebrews 5:8, 9.

Need for Spiritual Maturity

Introduction. Throughout this chapter the author continues his parenthetical remarks which he began in Hebrews 5:11 about the condition of the people to whom he writes. This section includes warnings and exhortations for the Christian.

Hebrews 6:1-8

1. What is the exhortation which the writer gives here to the people described at the end of chapter 5? Why does he use the pronoun *us?* Why is progress essential? *Perfection* (King James Version) is used in the sense of maturity. Look up *maturity* in the dictionary. Whom do you consider mature as a Christian? Why?

2. List the basic doctrines of the early church mentioned in verses 1, 2. Read these verses from several translations. What was every young Christian expected to understand and to do?

3. What necessary and sobering qualification does the writer recognize in verse 3?

4. The verb in the expression *let us go on* in verse 1 is passive, and the same as that used in 2 Peter 1:21 to describe the writing of Scripture. The writer actually is saying *let us be borne along* to maturity. Personal surrender, not effort, is the primary meaning. How can we yield ourselves to the power of God? See Philippians 2:13; Ephesians 3:20, 21.

5. With what people (verses 4-8) is it pointless to return to basic doctrines? Why?

6. What five privileges have those people had who are described in verses 4, 5? State the meaning of these blessings in your own words.

7. Verse 6 speaks of *falling away* or *committing apostasy*, which the dictionary defines as "abandonment of what one has voluntarily professed." How is apostasy similar to the action of those who put Jesus to death (verse 6)? How does it bring contempt upon him?

8. What is the point of the illustration from nature in verses 7, 8? When does judgment come? Why?

9. This is one of the most solemn portions of the New Testament. What does it reveal about our Christian faith and salvation?

Hebrews 6:9-12

10. The author here addresses his readers as *beloved*, the only place in the letter that he does so. Why, do you think, does this expression of love come particularly at this point? Why are we most stern with those whom we really love?

11. Why does the writer have confidence concerning those to whom he writes? What evidence is there that they have not fallen into apostasy, though they are harshly described in 5:11-14?

12. Consider the importance of the expression *each of you* (verse 11). Why must Christians never treat people as a part of the masses, but rather as persons? What does the writer desire for each one?

13. In verses 10-12 for what are these Christians commended? To what are they encouraged? Against what are they warned?

14. How is the faith and patience of others who have succeeded spiritually both an encouragement and a pattern for us? What have you read lately which has helped you learn about the type of person described in verse 12?

Hebrews 6:13-20

15. See Genesis 17:19; 21:1, 2, 5; 22:1, 2, 12, 13, 15-18. How is Abraham an example of those *who through faith and patience inherit the promises?* What is there to encourage us as we review God's dealings with Abraham? What qualities did Abraham exhibit?

16. What double basis for confidence in the truth and sure

fulfillment of his promise did God give to Abraham (Hebrews 6:13-18)? What exactly was the promise given to Abraham (Genesis 22:17, 18)? This promise came true in Jesus Christ.

17. What is unchangeable here (verses 17, 18)? Why should this be an encouragement to Christians who are the spiritual children of Abraham, *heirs of the promise?*

18. What word pictures are drawn in verses 19, 20? What is the function of an anchor? How then is an anchor a suitable illustration of Christian hope? How is Jesus linked to this hope? What has Jesus done for us as our high priest?

Note — Verse 19, *that within the veil* or *the inner shrine behind the curtain* — refers to the holy of holies in the Old Testament tabernacle (temple) into which the high priest of Israel went once a year on the day of atonement, sprinkling the blood of animals on the mercy seat to make atonement for himself and all Israel. (For details, see Exodus 26:33, 34; Leviticus 16:11-19.)

SUMMARY

1. Find what you think is the spiritual low point of this chapter. What do you consider the spiritual high point of the chapter? Why?

2. What does this chapter teach about hope? What are we exhorted to do about this hope? See verses 11, 18, 19.

3. From this study, what are the characteristics which a true Christian should emulate?

APPLICATION

Most of this chapter is devoted to a parenthesis expressing the writer's concern for his fellow Christians. The severity of the warning in verses 4-6 should make each of us seriously consider his own spiritual condition. This week spend time in private prayer about this.

Memorize Hebrews 6:19, 20.

Hebrews 7

Melchizedek

Introduction. In this chapter the writer returns to the thought of Hebrews 5:11, the meaning of the Melchizedek priesthood of Jesus. He shows the importance of the fact that Jesus, like Melchizedek, is King and Priest.

Hebrews 7:1-3

1. Read Genesis 14:17-20 and Psalm 110:4 for the Old Testament background on Melchizedek.

2. List all the points made about Melchizedek in verses 1-3.

3. Remembering that Jesus is compared to Melchizedek, what is significant about the meaning of Melchizedek's name and the name of the place of his reign? What comparison is drawn between Melchizedek and Jesus in verse 3?

Hebrews 7:4-10

4. What things prove the greatness of Melchizedek? What contrasts are drawn with the Levitical priesthood? How is Melchizedek shown to be superior to the Levitical priesthood in at least three ways?

5. What argument does the writer use to demonstrate that the whole Levitical priesthood is inferior to Melchizedek?

Hebrews 7:11-19

6. Note — *the order of Aaron* — Aaron, a member of the tribe of Levi and the brother of Moses, was the first high priest of Israel. The Levitical priesthood was made up only of the direct descendants of Aaron, while the men called Levites who helped these priests in the temple, though not of Aaron's

family, had to be members of the tribe of Levi.

What is the point of the question in verse 11? How does the writer argue that the Levitical priesthood was defective and not intended to be permanent? Why was the Levitical priesthood necessary under the law? See 5:1-3. What does the change in the priesthood reveal about the way a man now has access to God?

7. To whom does verse 17 (Psalm 110:4) refer? Compare the requirements for the Melchizedek priesthood with those of the Levitical priesthood. See Hebrews 5:4-6, 8-10; 7:15-17. What is the essential requirement now rather than physical descent? What does the term *indestructible life* (*endless life*) suggest about the power of the priest in Melchizedek's likeness?

8. To what two great conclusions does the author arrive in verses 18 and 19? What has been canceled? What has been introduced? Why?

9. What is the meaning of the expression, *a better hope?* What is now possible for the first time for sinful man? See also 4:14, 16.

Hebrews 7:20-28

10. What two further proofs are set forth to show that the priesthood of Jesus after the order of Melchizedek is superior to the Levitical priesthood under the law?

11. A covenant is essentially an agreement between two parties. The old covenant between the people of Israel and God is described in Exodus 24:1-8, especially verses 3 and 7. From Hebrews 7 what evidence is there that the new covenant is better than the old?

12. Why was there no permanence in the old priesthood? How is the fact emphasized that Jesus is forever the only way to God? What specifically does Jesus do in his continuing ministry? For whom?

13. Define the terms used to describe Jesus in verse 26. How does Jesus, our high priest, meet our needs?

Note — *Holy* refers to how Jesus stands before God; *blameless* can be translated "never hurt any man." For how Jesus was different from sinners (*undefiled* and *separate*) in verse 26, see 2:18; 4:15; 5:8, 9.

14. What further contrasts are drawn in verses 27, 28 between the priesthood of Jesus and that of the Old Testament high priests? What did they do that he never had to do? What did he do which they never did?

15. Describe at least three ways in which the two *appointments* of verse 28 are different?

SUMMARY

1. How does Jesus bring a better hope (verse 19) and a better covenant (verse 22)?

2. What old ways have been done away with? Why?

3. Turn to the chart of this book on page 10 and locate today's study portion in the framework of the letter. We have now finished the second major section of the book, in which Jesus is shown to be our great high priest, not after the order of Aaron but after the order of Melchizedek. Continue to fill in your own observations of warnings, contrasts, "therefore's" and Old Testament quotations found in these chapters.

APPLICATION

If you have always worshiped in churches in which liturgy and the sacraments are not emphasized, consider especially the great truth of the high priesthood of Jesus Christ on your behalf. Meditate on this, and let this truth affect your prayers this week. If you do come from a liturgical church, take a fresh look at how the rituals in which you take part express the truth of the high priesthood of Jesus Christ on your behalf.

Memorize Hebrews 7:26, 27.

Hebrews 8

The Real Sanctuary
and the Better Covenant

Introduction. The high priest of Israel functioned in a sanctuary and under the specifications of a covenant which enabled him to come before God with animal sacrifices for the sins of the people.

Hebrews 8:1-5

1. *Such a high priest* (verse 1) refers to the description of Jesus given in chapters 6 and 7. Summarize briefly this description of our high priest (6:19, 20; 7:15-28).

2. In verses 1, 2 the writer comes to the main point of his letter. What does he affirm about Jesus here? Compare 6:19, 20 with 8:1, 2.

3. Why doesn't Jesus carry on his high priestly work on earth? How does 8:3 recall the teaching in 7:27?

4. Compare by listing in two parallel columns the points made in verses 1-5 about the location and function of the earthly sanctuary and of the heavenly sanctuary, and the identity and function of the priest(s) in each.

What is the relationship of the earthly sanctuary to the heavenly? Which is the real sanctuary and which is the reproduction (or copy)? How do God's instructions to Moses quoted in verse 5 substantiate this?

Hebrews 8:6-13

5. In verse 6 what is better than what? The work of Christ (verse 6) is described as mediation. What does this mean?

6. Why is the work of Christ superior to the work of the high priest done under the old covenant?

7. How does the writer account for a second or new cove-

nant? What does he prove by the quotation in verses 8-12 from Jeremiah 31:31-34?

8. In what specific ways, according to Jeremiah's prophecy, would the new covenant differ from the old?

9. Contrast the relationship between God and his people revealed in verse 9 and verse 12. Upon what did each covenant depend for success? Why is this difference so important?

10. Compare the words of Jesus in John 6:44, 45 with the point being made in verse 11. Why is there no spiritually privileged class under the new covenant as there was under the old? Why does access to God not depend now upon keeping the law, or power, money, position, or education? Why does each of these fail to give men access to God?

11. Compare the way in which the old covenant was transmitted to the people through Moses with the way the new covenant was transmitted (verse 10). What difference does this make?

12. How were sins dealt with under the old covenant? See Hebrews 7:27; 5:1. What is to be done about sin according to the promises of the new covenant? Upon whose character and action does salvation now solely depend?

13. In verse 13 what conclusions does the writer draw from the fact that this new covenant was spoken of by the prophet Jeremiah?

SUMMARY

1. Why are religious rituals not sufficient for our spiritual need? Of what value are they?

2. To what extent are the promises of Jeremiah 31:31-34 *better promises* than those of the old covenant? Why?

3. How does Jesus mediate the new covenant described by Jeremiah? See also Matthew 26:28.

APPLICATION

What *do* you do when you are overwhelmed with a sense of sin, failure, guilt, depression? What *should* you do? Apply to your own life all that is available to you because of the mediation of the Lord Jesus Christ.

REVIEW Hebrews 7:26, 27. Memorize Hebrews 8:1.

Hebrews 9

The Blood of the Covenant

(Because of its length, you may wish to do this study in two sessions.)

Introduction. In this chapter there is an explanation of the events of the Day of Atonement and their meaning. Contrasted with this, the work of Christ is shown to be the perfect sacrifice which alone can give us access to God.

Hebrews 9:1-10

1. What two things (verse 1) were necessary under the first covenant? What do you learn about the furnishings of the tabernacle in verses 1-5? To what part of the tabernacle is attention specially drawn?

(Note — For a detailed account of the tabernacle read in preparation for this study, Exodus chapters 25 through 31, and chapters 35 through 40.)

2. What were the duties of the priests in the tabernacle (verses 6, 7)? In what parts of the tabernacle did the ordinary priests carry on their activity? the high priest? How often? See also Leviticus 16:32-34.

3. The activities of the tabernacle service were directed to the purpose of enabling men to draw near to God, but what did the great difficulty of access into the Holy of Holies reveal, according to verse 8?

(Note — *Sanctuary* or *holiest of all* here means the immediate presence of God.)

4. With what did gifts and sacrifices offered in the tabernacle deal? In what area were these sacrifices ineffective? Why

is ritual holiness which is gained by ceremony only a temporary and shadowy copy of the real? How does verse 10 reiterate the conclusion stated in 8:13?

Hebrews 9:11-14

5. According to verses 11, 12, when did the time of reformation mentioned in verse 10 occur?

6. List in two parallel columns what you observe in verses 6-14 about the service and sacrifices of the first covenant and the service and sacrifice of Christ. How do they differ in their nature and in their results? How are these differences significant?

7. What two things does the blood of Christ (verses 12, 14) do that animals' blood could not do? What practical difference does this make to you?

Hebrews 9:15-22

8. (Note — In verses 15, 16 the same Greek word is translated both as *covenant* (verse 15) and *testament* or *will* (verse 16).)

Why did Christ have to die? What two reasons are set forth in verses 15-22? When does a will become operative? Who receives an eternal inheritance? How?

9. Note how verse 15 indicates that Christ's death was retroactively effective for those who lived under the old covenant. Compare with Romans 3:24, 25.

10. Read Exodus 24:6-8 and Leviticus 17:11. What part did blood play under the law? What conclusion is drawn in Hebrews 9:22? Why is blood so valuable? Why does the forgiveness of man's sins cost so much? Compare with Romans 3:21-26, especially verses 25b, 26.

11. Think of examples in human relationships when forgiveness costs someone a great deal. Why is forgiveness perhaps the most costly commodity in the world?

Hebrews 9:23-28

12. What two arguments are set forth in verses 24-26 to illustrate the point made in verse 23 about *better sacrifices?*

13. How are sins taken away? Why does no work of ours

have to be added, nor does the work of Christ have to be repeated?

14. What is the point made by the final contrast in this chapter between the death of all other men and the death of Christ (verses 27, 28)? See Mark 10:45. What is the warning and what is the promise?

15. What does Christ's second coming mean to those whose love for him makes them eager to see him? What does his coming mean for the unbeliever?

SUMMARY

1. Note the many references in this chapter to blood and to Christ's death. What does this reveal about the way in which sin is forgiven and the way that man obtains access to God?

2. What good did the worship and sacrifices under the first covenant do? How were they performed? *How much more* (verse 14) is available now because of what Christ has done? Why?

APPLICATION

The heart of the message of the book of Hebrews is found in the large section starting with chapter 8 and concluding with 10:18. A major part of this teaching is found in chapter 9. If you have never understood the meaning of the crucifixion, if you have never before appropriated Christ's death on your behalf, do so now in prayer. Think about the warning in Hebrews 2:3 and the promise in 9:28.

Memorize Hebrews 9:25, 26.

Hebrews 10

The Perfection
of Christ's Sacrifice
Personal Application

(Because of its length, you may wish to study this chapter in two sessions.)

Introduction. This chapter concludes the theological argument of the letter by describing the perfections of the offering of Jesus Christ for sins. It begins the section on how we should live in the light of his sacrifice on our behalf.

Hebrews 10:1-10

1. In what three ways (verses 1, 2, 4) did the sacrifices of the Old Testament tabernacle prove inadequate? What reasons are given for the failures of the law and its animal sacrifices?

2. Because of the situation just described in verses 1-4, what does the Messiah (Christ) say about his coming into this world (verses 5-7)? How does this use of Psalm 40:6-8 indicate what God really wants?

Compare with similar expressions of this thought in the Old Testament as found in 1 Samuel 15:22; Psalm 51:16, 17; Hosea 6:6; Micah 6:6-8. Why is full obedience the only true sacrifice and the only way acceptable to God? Illustrate the importance of obedience from family life.

3. What conclusion does the writer of this letter draw (verses 8, 9) as to the meaning of the quotation in verses 5-7? What significance does he see in the order of the statements in the Psalm?

4. What was the *will* of God (verses 7, 10) that Christ accomplished through his *body* (verses 5, 10)?

5. How are we cleansed from sin and made holy and acceptable to God? What did Jesus Christ do that no other man could do (verse 10)?

Hebrews 10:11-18

6. With this paragraph the writer concludes the theological argument he began in chapter 1. How does he summarize the differences between the old and the new way? Find as many differences as you can between the Old Testament priests and Christ. Why are each of these differences important to us?

(Note — *Sanctified* in verse 10 means to be forever made fit for God's presence and set apart for his service.)

7. From 10:15 and 9:8 what do you learn about the ministry of the Holy Spirit? See also John 14:26; 16:13.

8. Why doesn't the sacrifice that Jesus made need to be repeated (verses 10, 12, 14)? How does the quotation from Jeremiah 31:33, 34 substantiate this (verses 16-18)?

9. Refer to the chart of this book on page 10. You will note that we have now come to the end of the third major section of the letter at 10:18. Review briefly the main thoughts of this section. Add to your written observations on the chart, noting especially the contrasts involved, the arguments presented, and Old Testament quotations used.

(Divide the study at this point if you wish to do it in two sessions.)

Hebrews 10:19-25

10. There are a number of important points in this passage. Find three things stated about Jesus. Find at least three things we are urged to do in the light of these truths about Jesus. (Compare with Hebrews 4:14-16.) Find three practical suggestions concerning our responsibilities to our fellow Christians.

11. Another way of approaching this section (verses 19-25) is to note the following: What is to be the Christian's relationship to God? What is stated about his witness to the world? What is his responsibility to his fellow Christians?

12. With verse 20, compare the events of Matthew 27:50, 51. How do we now have access to God? How should this access affect practically our daily lives?

13. In verses 24, 25 what reasons are given for going to church and to other Christian meetings? To what extent are these purposes accomplished in your church gatherings?

14. What coming event gives urgency to the exhortations in verses 24, 25? With verse 25 compare Matthew 24:14, 27, 30, 31, 44.

Hebrews 10:26-31

15. In contrast to the great blessings of a life of faith, hope, and love described in verses 19-25, what is the terrible warning of this section, particularly as stated in verses 26, 27? What does *deliberately* or *willfully* (verse 26) suggest about this sin?

16. What three phrases are used in verse 29 to describe the deliberate sin mentioned in verse 26? Put into your own words these things which describe in essence the sin of apostasy. Why does the writer conjecture a far worse punishment for apostasy now than in Moses' time?

17. What do the quotations from Deuteronomy in verse 30 tell us about the nature of God's holiness? Why is the warning in verse 31 necessary?

Hebrews 10:32-39

18. Having given his readers this severe warning, to what does the writer now draw their attention? What had these Christians experienced? Why? How had they reacted? Why?

19. What advice does the writer give in the light of their former conduct and attitude? Specifically, what two things are advised and what results are promised?

20. Following a pattern he has used throughout the letter, the writer quotes from the Old Testament to back up the points just made. How does the quotation from Habakkuk in verses 37, 38 lend weight to what the writer has been saying in verses 19-36? Describe the two choices with which the chapter concludes. Which choice are you making?

SUMMARY

1. Summarize the theological arguments presented in 10:1-18.

2. What practical advice is given in 10:19-39 to those who live under the new covenant?

APPLICATION

Make a list of personal resolutions in the light of the warnings and promises in this chapter. What are you going to do about your spiritual life? How can you test and strengthen your spiritual health?

Memorize Hebrews 10:19-22.

The Superiority of Faith

(This chapter may be studied in two sessions.)

Introduction. The great examples of faith in this chapter illustrate the quality of response which God expects from man. The author continues his exhortations to those who have benefited by the blood of Jesus and have received access to God through him.

Because the Old Testament incidents alluded to in this chapter may be unfamiliar to many, it is important that everyone allow ample time in advance study preparation to *read the background references before* coming to the group discussion. In this way, the group discussion can deal with the points the writer of this letter intended to make by alluding to these Old Testament incidents.

Hebrews 11:1-7

1. Review the emphasis given to faith in Hebrews 10:38, 39. Read 11:1 from several different translations. How is faith defined here? Note that faith deals with things future and things invisible. What did confidence in God's promises, and acting on this confidence do for the Old Testament heroes (verse 2)?

2. What understanding about the universe does faith give us? See also Psalm 33:6, 7. What does our realization that this is God's world do for us in all circumstances?

3. What can you learn from the example of Abel's faith? How did Abel's sacrifice (Genesis 4:3-5) foreshadow the sacrifice of Christ in a way which Cain's sacrifice did not? See

Hebrews 9:22, 26b. What influence does Abel's sacrifice to God continue to have? Why?

4. For **background** on verse 5 see Genesis 5:21-24. What great principle concerning faith (verse 6) is drawn from Enoch's example? What two things are essential for a man to believe if he would approach God? Why?

5. For **background** on Noah see Genesis 6:5-22. Consider the pressures which Noah must have faced, tempting him to ignore the warning of God. What pressures are there on your faith? What effects did Noah's faith have?

6. Why do Abel, Enoch, and Noah all share the standing of *righteous* before God? In what differing ways did these three men express their faith in God (verses 4, 5, 7)? Yet what factor was common to the lives of all three men?

Hebrews 11:8-22

7. What verbs describe Abraham's faith in action? What changes did such faith bring into Abraham's life? What degree of faith did Sarah have? Why was she able to believe the incredible? How has the faith of Abraham and Sarah affected us all?

8. How is the experience of the faithful people mentioned thus far summarized in verses 13-16? Give a practical illustration of what it will mean in our attitudes and actions if we follow their example.

9. What is God's response to their faith (verse 16)? What picture of the life of faith is suggested here? Compare this with the concept of the life of faith which many people inside and outside the church have today.

10. What do all of the illustrations in verses 17-22 have in common concerning the degree of faith involved?

Hebrews 11:23-31

11. What five great acts of faith are described in verses 23-29? What specific things did Moses believe which influenced his actions (verses 24-28)?

12. Why would it have been particularly difficult to exercise faith in the instances mentioned in verses 29, 30?

13. For **background** on the incidents in verses 30, 31, see

Joshua 2:1-24; 6:1-25. What did Rahab believe that led her to help the Israelites? Note the place of Rahab in the genealogy of Christ (Matthew 1:5).

14. What tremendous results followed the exercise of faith in these instances?

Hebrews 11:32-40

15. In this section the writer to the Hebrews proceeds to touch on a wide range of incidents down through the centuries of Israel's history from their entry into the Promised Land through the times of the kingdom, the exile and return, and the then-recent period of the Maccabees between the Old and New Testaments.

How are verses 35-38 a contrast to verses 32-34? What great achievements were accomplished through faith (verses 32-35a)? What terrible sufferings were borne by faith (verses 35b-38)? Why are even the sufferings endured considered achievements as well as the obvious victories won?

16. According to verses 38, 39, what three things were true of all these victorious and suffering heroes who lived before the coming of Christ? Why did they not see the fulfilment of God's promises? What great challenge does this present to us who are Christians?

17. (Note — The reference to the sufferings in verses 35-38 is probably primarily to the terrible period between the Old and New Testaments when Antiochus Epiphanes, king of Syria, made a deliberate attempt to wipe out the Jewish religion, and the Maccabees at dreadful cost regained the freedom of the Jews.)

Consider the tremendous debt we as Christians owe to the faithful Jews who kept their faith in spite of these pressures in the centuries before Christ's coming.

SUMMARY

1. In verse 1, faith is shown essentially to deal with things future (*hoped for*) and things invisible (*not seen*). Look back over this chapter and note how each person's faith dealt with either future or invisible realities.

2. If you had never known anything about faith as it is

spoken of in the Bible, what would you conclude about it from this chapter alone?

3. What effect should this chapter have had upon its first readers? How is your life going to be different because you studied this chapter about faith?

4. What choices did the people described in this chapter face? What choices do you face? Be specific.

APPLICATION

If you exercise the kind of faith in Jesus Christ described in this chapter, take time this week to consider what it may cost you personally in terms of status, wealth, intellectual respectability, security, physical comfort, pleasures, or anything else in which you may be tempted to place your faith and values. Pray that you may so exercise your faith that you will receive divine approval (verse 1).

Memorize Hebrews 11:1, 6.

Hebrews 12

The Disciplined Life

Introduction. This chapter presents the challenge to live for Christ in the face of great difficulties, and reminds us of who God is and of what he is like.

Hebrews 12:1-11

1. To whom does the expression *so great a cloud of witnesses* refer? (See chapter 11.) Note that these people are witnesses in a double sense — they have borne their own confession of faith and they are now watching our performance. How should this be an inspiration to us?

2. What advice does the author give for running the race of this Christian life? Describe the hindrances we face and what we can do about them. Why is perseverance essential in this race?

3. List all the things revealed about Jesus in verses 2 and 3. What difference should these truths about Jesus make to the Christian? What challenge is laid down in verse 4?

4. The costliness of the Christian faith is not emphasized in many churches today. How is it costly to follow Christ? See also Mark 8:34, 35, 38.

5. Of what should the Proverbs quotation in verses 5, 6 remind the readers of this letter? What is the meaning of suffering, and its purpose for the Christian?

6. Trace the line of reasoning in verses 5-11. Why should discipline be expected? How should discipline be accepted? What benefits may result? For whom? For what *the peaceful fruit of righteousness* means, read verse 11 in several recent translations. Put the definition in your own words.

7. What contrast is drawn between the discipline of earthly fathers and the discipline of our Heavenly Father (verses 9, 10)? Why should this make a difference in how we respond to suffering? Discuss the different ways in which one can respond to the discipline which the Lord gives. How ought the Christian to respond to such discipline?

Hebrews 12:12-17

8. Picture in your mind the persons addressed in verses 12, 13. What impression do you get? What counsel is given and what danger is mentioned?

Suggest practical ways in which we may help one another to do what verses 12, 13 recommend. Compare with Romans 15:1, 2. Why do people sometimes get *out of joint (disabled)* spiritually?

9. What two aims are suggested in verse 14? With what two relationships do they deal? Note the use of the verb *strive* or *try*. How can we do this? Why is *holiness* essential? (Note — The root meaning of *holy* is "different" or "separate.") Why can't the true Christian follow the world's standards?

10. Describe the dangers to the Christian life outlined in verses 15 and 16. The term *root of bitterness* comes from Deuteronomy 29:18 and refers to a person who follows false gods and encourages others to do so, thereby becoming a poisonous, corrupting influence on other Christians.

11. What tests can you suggest to make sure that you, your family, your church, are not infected by idolatry? What can be done if there is a *root of bitterness* in your life?

12. How does Esau illustrate the tragic results of rejecting God's blessings? What value standard did Esau exhibit? Why did he weep?

Hebrews 12:18-24

13. Read Deuteronomy 4:11-13 and Exodus 19:12, 13 for a description of the events at the giving of the law on Mount Sinai to which Hebrews 12:8-21 refers. What impressions do these three passages give of what it was like to approach God at Mt. Sinai? What reactions did men have? What did the experience at Mount Sinai reveal about God?

14. Contrast the experience of the Christian (verses 22-24) with that of the man approaching God under the old covenant (verses 18-21). What do those have who come to Mount Zion? Why need we not fear as Moses did? What does it mean that Jesus is the mediator of the new covenant? Compare Hebrews 8:6 and 1 Timothy 2:5, 6.

15. What was the result of Abel's death? See Genesis 4: 8-12. In contrast, what was the result of Jesus' death? See also Romans 5:8, 9.

Hebrews 12:25-29

16. Sum up in your own words the warning with which this chapter concludes, and the reasons given for this warning.

17. Since we have been given a part in the eternal kingdom of God which will outlast the shaking of earth and heaven, what ought to characterize our lives and our worship? With verse 28 compare Romans 12:1, 2.

SUMMARY

1. Describe in your own words the Christian life as pictured in this chapter. What should the Christian remember? What should he do? Of what should he beware?

2. From this study what would you say is the truly Christian view of suffering and trouble?

3. What is revealed in this chapter about God?

APPLICATION

Set aside one-half hour for quiet meditation and commit your present troubles and difficulties to the Lord, praying that he may use them in your life to bring forth the righteous life as promised in Hebrews 12:11.

Memorize Hebrews 12:1, 2.

Hebrews 13

Practical Expressions of the Christian Life

Introduction. This chapter contains specific advice for the Christian in terms of the responsibilities he has to others. The chapter and the book conclude with one of the great benedictions of the New Testament.

Hebrews 13:1-6

1. Find the five qualities which should characterize the Christian in everyday life, as described in verses 1-6.

2. What, do you think, are the major pitfalls to brotherly love existing in the church today? How can we change our attitudes if we tend to be critical, fault-finding, and unsympathetic?

3. To whom is it recommended that we especially show hospitality? Why? What evidence of Christian hospitality have you seen expressed? To what "strangers" do you have opportunities (if you seek them) to extend hospitality? What about students from overseas at a nearby college, young people who need a sponsor for their church group, lonely older people in convalescent or retirement homes?

4. Why were many Christians at the time of this letter often in prison or persecuted in other ways? Consider the risk involved for those who associate with outcasts at any time in history. What price are we prepared to pay to express our allegiance to our fellow-Christians?

5. Discuss briefly the challenges to sexual purity which we face today. What is God's clear command concerning sexual relationships (verse 4)?

6. What does a lack of contentment indicate about a per-

son? How do we express discontent? What reasons for being content does the writer emphasize by using the two Old Testament quotations in verses 5 and 6? See also Matthew 6:31-33. Give some practical suggestions as to how to raise children so that they have the best opportunity to keep their lives free from *the love of* money.

Hebrews 13:7-16

7. How are true spiritual leaders described (verse 7)? When we know such leaders, how should we allow them to influence us? What perspective does verse 8 give concerning all earthly leaders? Why is only Jesus' leadership permanent?

8. According to verse 9, about what were the early Christians in danger of being confused? Why is it easy to slip into overstressing rituals, food laws, or the like, as a means to spiritual strength and reality? How is a Christian strengthened spiritually?

9. What argument is set forth in verses 9-12? Based on that argument, what six things (verses 13-16) does the writer conclude we should do? How do these attitudes and actions express the true meaning of sacrifice?

10. In what ways may you have to bear abuse or reproach for your allegiance to the Lord Jesus Christ?

11. How are we to offer a sacrifice of praise to God (verse 15)?

12. Compare verse 16 with Matthew 25:37-40. In light of these verses, what practical actions ought you to take?

Hebrews 13:17-25

13. What duty does a congregation have to its leaders? Why? Compare verse 17 with 3 John 4 for insight into the attitude of a true spiritual leader.

14. What does the writer want his readers to pray for him (verses 18, 19)?

15. In your own words, what does the writer of this letter pray that God will do *for* his readers, and do *in* them (verses 20, 21)? Turn this prayer into a prayer for yourself to be prayed at the end of this study session.

16. Compare verse 20 with John 10:10-18. What has Jesus

done to be called *the great shepherd of the sheep?* Do you belong to his flock and enjoy the fullness of life that he gives?

17. What is the author's personal plea in verse 22? Considering the majesty of his themes, he has dealt with them briefly, as he claims.

18. What is the personal message with which the letter closes?

SUMMARY

1. Describe the kind of Christian life discussed in this chapter. Name the specific points made here which you feel need to be emphasized in the life of Christians today. Suggest practical ways in which this may be done.

2. Refer to the chart of this letter on page 10. Note how what Jesus has done in providing access to God for us (Hebrews 1:1 through 10:18) leads to the *therefore* with which the final section of the letter begins in 10:19. On the basis of all that Christ has accomplished, what are we to do, and what qualities are to characterize our lives?

3. Use the prayer you have made (see question 15) as the closing prayer for this study.

APPLICATION

Practice offering a sacrifice of praise to God at least once a day for the next week. Be sure to make some of this praise audible, not just silent prayer.

Memorize Hebrews 13:20, 21. During the coming week, review all the verses from Hebrews that you have memorized, and think through the letter by using these verses as a framework.

RECOMMENDED PROGRAMS
FOR SMALL GROUP DISCUSSION BIBLE STUDY

New Groups and Outreach Groups
Mark (recommended as first unit of study)
Acts
John, Book 1 (Chapters 1-10)
John, Book 2 (Chapters 11-21)
Romans
Four Men of God (Abraham, Joseph, Moses, David)
1 and 2 Peter (Letters to People in Trouble)
Genesis (Chapters 1-13)

Groups Reaching People from Non-Christian Cultures
Genesis (Chapters 1-13)
Mark
Romans
Four Men of God (Abraham, Joseph, Moses, David)
Philippians and Colossians (Letters from Prison)
Patterns for Living with God (Twelve Old Testament Character Studies)

Church Groups
Genesis (Chapters 1-13)
Matthew, Book 1 (Chapters 1-16)
Matthew, Book 2 (Chapters 17-28)
1 Corinthians (Challenge to Maturity)
2 Corinthians and Galatians (A Call for Help and Freedom)
1 and 2 Peter (Letters to People in Trouble)
Psalms and Proverbs
Four Men of God (Abraham, Joseph, Moses, David)
Celebrate

Mission Concerns Groups
Luke
Acts
Ephesians and Philemon
The Coming of the Lord (1 and 2 Thessalonians, 2 and 3 John, Jude)
Romans
1 John and James
Amos (Prophet of Life-Style)

Advanced Groups
Courage to Cope
They Met Jesus (Eight Studies of New Testament Characters)
Hebrews
Choose Life (Ten Studies of Basic Christian Doctrines)
Amos (Prophet of Life-Style)
The Coming of the Lord (1 and 2 Thessalonians, 2 and 3 John, Jude)
Prophets of Hope (Haggai, Zechariah, Malachi)

Sunday School (Adult and older teens)
Matthew, Book 1 (Chapters 1-16)
Matthew, Book 2 (Chapters 17-28)
They Met Jesus (Eight Studies of New Testament Characters)
Choose Life (Ten Studies of Basic Christian Doctrines)
Celebrate
Courage to Cope
Set Free
Patterns for Living with God (Twelve Old Testament Character Studies)

Biweekly or Monthly Groups
They Met Jesus (Eight Studies of New Testament Characters)
Set Free
Celebrate
Courage to Cope
Psalms and Proverbs

How to Start a Neighborhood Bible Study
(A Guide to Discussion Study) is also available.